UNVEILING TECH DEBT

UNVEILING TECH DEBT

*A Business Leaders Guide
to Measuring and Managing
Enterprise Tech Debt Leverage*

DR. KEN KNAPTON

bridgewood publishing

An Imprint of Cedar Fort, Inc.
Springville, Utah

Some content and images shared with IDC with permission.

Published by Bridgewood Publishing, an imprint of Cedar Fort, Inc.
2373 W. 700 S., Springville, UT 84663

Printed in the United States of America

10 9 8 7 6 5 4 3 2 1

Printed on acid-free paper

Contents

Chapter 1

UNDERSTANDING ENTERPRISE TECH DEBT

During the 2022 holiday travel season, Southwest Airlines experienced a technology failure that affected 2 million customers and resulted in the cancelation of 16,900 flights, an immediate 16% drop in their stock price, an over $800 million loss that fiscal year, and a $140 million fine assessed more than a year later.[1] Significant winter storms that year had disrupted air travel across the United States and forced airlines to cancel flights and scramble to re-book their customers. While other airlines recovered in a matter of days, Southwest Airlines took weeks to return to normal activity. Their recovery from this event was significantly hampered because of their legacy IT systems. Their technology team had known for quite some time that their systems needed upgrades and critical maintenance, but this work was never given priority or funding.

In 2017, Equifax suffered a data breach that exposed the records of more than 150 million customers. The breach occurred because Equifax had failed to remediate known security vulnerabilities within their enterprise systems, and because they failed to implement a critical security patch that may have prevented the breach. Both the Southwest outage and the Equifax breach were avoidable. Both were the result of technical debt within their enterprise systems.

In the rapidly evolving landscape of the modern business world, technology has emerged as both a driving force and a potential Achilles' heel. Both Southwest Airlines and Equifax relied on their enterprise systems to accomplish daily operational activities that kept their revenue engines running, yet those systems failed them in significant ways. These two examples are not uncommon stories. Organizations, regardless of their industry or size, have become increasingly reliant on technology to streamline operations, engage customers, and gain a competitive edge. These activities are colloquially referred to by the much-overused term "digital transformation." As technology becomes ubiquitous in all aspects of consumers' lives, companies must evolve to include technological solutions to everything from the customer experience to the employee workflow. Yet, as companies journey deeper into this digital age, a subtle and often underestimated adversary lurks in the shadows—enterprise tech debt.

In this book I will embark on a quest to unveil the intricacies of enterprise tech debt—a concept that extends far beyond the realm of custom software development. I will explore tech debt from its beginning as a construct in the agile world of custom software development to its evolving nature as applied across the entire infrastructure of an enterprise, and will discuss why it has become a critical concern for organizations worldwide. Finally,

I will provide real solutions for companies looking for ways to measure and manage their enterprise tech debt. Before we get too much farther, we need to consider the humble beginnings of the term "tech debt" and explain what "enterprise tech debt" means in the context of the original coined phrase.

The Agile Origins of Tech Debt

The term "technical debt" or "tech debt" was initially coined in 1992 by Ward Cunningham, one of the founders of agile programming and one of the original authors of the Agile Manifesto. Cunningham introduced the concept of technical debt in a 1992 paper he wrote for the OOPSLA conference (Object-Oriented Programming, Systems, Languages & Applications). In that paper, Cunningham used the metaphor of financial debt to describe a common phenomenon in software development. He explained that when developers make decisions to expedite the delivery of software, they often take shortcuts or write suboptimal code. Thus, tech debt initially referred to the compromises made during software development—**decisions to favor short-term gains over long-term sustainability**. These shortcuts, analogous to financial debt, accumulate interest over time, resulting in a metaphorical "debt" that must eventually be repaid. Just as financial debt accrues interest over time, technical debt accrues "interest" in the form of **increased complexity**, **reduced maintainability**, and **potentially higher costs** in the future. In its earliest form, tech debt was synonymous with coding shortcuts—hasty decisions that aimed to meet deadlines but often led to messy, difficult-to-maintain codebases. This concept of technical debt resonated with software developers and became a valuable metaphor for explaining the trade-offs involved in software development. It highlighted the importance of balancing short-term gains with long-term sustainability and quality. Agile practitioners recognized that tech debt was an integral part of software development, necessitating a balance between rapid delivery and code quality.

Tech debt also had a negative connotation for some agile practitioners who used it as a derogatory term, as evidenced in this definition from an academic study: "Technical debt describes the consequences of software development actions that intentionally or unintentionally prioritize client value and/or project constraints, such as delivery deadlines, over more technical implementation, and design considerations."[2] Tech debt has also been seen to inhibit innovation, as explained here: "Technical debt is not merely a 'house-cleaning' chore; it is a fundamental issue that works like an anchor to slow down any tech-driven initiative. Companies that take the time to address it thoughtfully and carefully will be the ones best able to harness technology to drive revenue and innovation at scale."[3]

Beyond Code: The Rise of Enterprise Tech Debt

Over time, the idea of technical debt expanded beyond code to encompass broader technology-related decisions within organizations, giving rise to the concept of "enterprise tech debt."

Organizations began to realize that tech debt was not confined to code alone. It permeated every facet of their technological ecosystems, from outdated infrastructure to cumbersome data management practices, from unwieldy third-party integrations to the seductive allure of "quick fixes" that accumulated over time. This extension recognizes that tech debt can also manifest in infrastructure, architectural choices, data management, and even the use of third-party software solutions.

Today, both technical debt and enterprise tech debt are widely discussed in the technology industry, and they play a crucial role in shaping how organizations approach software development and technology management. The concept remains a fundamental part of agile methodologies and software engineering practices, emphasizing the need to continuously invest in maintaining and improving technology to prevent the accumulation of debt that can hinder an organization's progress. Enterprises today grapple not only with the tech debt rooted in custom code but also with a more expansive and insidious foe—enterprise tech debt. This is where the distinction arises, transcending the confines of code and infiltrating every facet of an organization's technological ecosystem.

In this book, I will attempt to shed some light on how traditional tech debt is just one piece of a much larger puzzle. Beyond code, it encompasses infrastructure, software-as-a-service (SaaS) solutions, data management, and any technological element that stands in the way of an enterprise's progress toward its strategic goals. My goal here is to unravel the intricacies of enterprise tech debt, making it comprehensible to key stakeholders—CIOs, CEOs, CFOs, and board members. My hope is to equip these executives with the knowledge and tools necessary to not only understand the profound impact of enterprise tech debt but also explain how to measure and manage it effectively within their organizations. I also aim to enlarge the concept of tech debt by adding an enterprise scope and calling it enterprise tech debt, and to introduce the concept of tech debt leverage before ending with an explanation of an algorithm that can be easily applied to any company and every enterprise to create a common language for discussing enterprise tech debt leverage with the executives and board of directors.

The definition of tech debt is evolving to include **all aspects of the tech stack** within an organization, thus the addition of the word "enterprise" in our discussion of tech debt as presented in this book. From this point on, the terms "enterprise tech debt" and "tech debt" will be used interchangeably throughout this book.

The consequences of enterprise tech debt extend far beyond code quality. They encompass hidden IT costs, increased operational risks, compromised security, hindered innovation, and challenges in adapting to change. Tech debt has evolved into a multifaceted challenge that demands the attention of leaders, from the CIOs responsible for technology strategy to the CEOs focused on the organization's bottom line. Time-to-market decisions can cause tech debt to accumulate across the entire infrastructure in the same way that it does for custom code. Using this definition, enterprise tech debt is also not always the result of poor decisions; it can easily accumulate within an enterprise as the result of a rapidly changing technology stack and extremely interconnected business-critical systems. The more tightly coupled enterprise systems are, the more prone they become to enterprise tech debt and the more challenging they become to update due to the interconnected interfaces, sharing of data, and intertwined data pathways. Thus, the maintenance, support, and improvement of these tightly coupled, critical business systems become much more challenging and expensive, and often get deprioritized in favor of more revenue-generating activities. This lack of maintenance is one of the factors of accumulating tech debt and increasing the tech debt leverage within an organization.

It is also important to note, however, that **enterprise tech debt is not always a bad thing**. Taking on some tech debt may be a strategic decision made after considering the various alternatives and business risks. Much like financial debt, tech debt could be the result of a conscious decision to move faster; some tech debt could be strategically leveraged to gain market share. For example, a decision may be made to delay the rollout of an upgrade to an aging ERP system to reduce the risk of interfering with a large sales opportunity that just arose. Alternatively, rolling out a new system with one of the main features disabled because one of the integrations was not ready at the same time all of the other capabilities were finished and tested may be warranted in order to hit a time-sensitive release window. In each case a business decision may be made to proceed because the sales opportunity is more time-sensitive than the ERP upgrade, or the missing integration is not as critical to the overall system as the rest of the capabilities. The former is an example of a decision to continue to carry tech debt beyond the initial plan, and the latter example is one where new tech debt would be incurred with the rollout of a new system. In both cases it would be important to plan for the tech debt payments to be made in the very near future. Just as financial leverage involves the use of borrowed capital to amplify investment returns, tech debt leverage involves utilizing technology to drive business growth.

I once worked with a healthcare company where one of the most business-critical components of their tech stack is the Electronic Health Records (EHR) system. This was at a critical time in the healthcare industry, as the entire landscape was changing from paper documentation and manual processes to a more digital approach. Each of the various providers, vendors, and medical offices defined their own digital transformation roadmap, and they were all trying to determine their part and/or responsibility in driving the healthcare industry into the digital future. To describe the environment as chaotic would be an understatement.

It was in this environment that this healthcare provider was working on an acquisition that would significantly increase the size of their business and bring with it much-needed improvement to their top line revenues. As the CIO responsible for all of the IT systems, I recognized that my primary responsibility was to ensure that all of the patient data was safe and protected, and that medical records remained intact and current. Because of the strict regulations regarding healthcare records and who could access them, we had to cut over the EHR at midnight on the date of the acquisition. It was a "big bang" transition, which is usually the least desirable way to transition major systems.

As we were evaluating the various components, vendors, and capabilities that all needed to be converted over to our system it became clear that one of the key integrations having to do with prescriptions would not be ready in time for the cutover. This meant that we would have to come up with a temporary solution, which was more of a manual process than the automated exchange we wanted to implement. The temporary solution meant more work on the part of the caregivers, and more possibility for human error to be introduced; however, the alternative was to miss the cutover date, which was simply not a realistic option.

This is a clear case of taking on tech debt to achieve a business outcome. The manual processes for prescriptions were not part of our long-term plan. Implementing even a temporary manual process meant training, configuring the system to handle the manual workflows, and additional operational costs involved with the paper processes, but we put the time and effort into making it work because it allowed us to meet a time-critical cutover in support of the timing of the acquisition Some people pointed out that we were expending effort on "throwaway" capabilities and wondered why we would put any time into building manual processes into our electronic health records system. They didn't recognize the regulatory and time constraints that went into the decision. To them it seemed like busywork that was going to be thrown out in just a few months. As an executive team, we made a conscious decision to take on some tech debt in order to meet a business goal, knowing that we would have to pay off that debt in just a few months. It was the right decision for the business.

Much like financial leverage, tech debt leverage carries risks, and managing it becomes paramount. Had we not gone back and automated the prescription process after the merger, we would have left the business in a less desirable technological position. We would have increased our tech debt leverage for little return. But knowing that we took on some new tech debt, we prioritized the effort to re-work the prescription process after the merger and automate it across our entire company.

This enterprise tech debt model provides a structured approach for leaders to engage in conversations such as this about tech debt, weighing the potential benefits and risks akin to the way they weigh financial decisions. Businesses often need to assume some financial debt to expand their company more quickly, and the same can be said for technological choices. A decision may be made to accept some technological risk resulting from the lack of updating a system in order to achieve a time-sensitive business opportunity. The challenges come when these decisions are made unconsciously, or without recognizing that tech debt is accumulating as a result of the specific business deci-sion. When technical decisions are made consciously with the understanding that some short-term trade-offs are being made in order to move more quickly in a specific direction, then the assumption of enterprise tech debt becomes a strategic decision made to benefit the company. When the accumulation of tech debt is not well understood, it easily becomes a problem that inhibits business growth at some point in the future.

As with high financial leverage, the problem with tech debt arises when it accumulates without making technological payments against that debt over time, thus increasing the leverage rather than reducing it. As companies become more digital, they need to actively measure and manage their tech debt leverage in the same way that they pay attention to their financial debt leverage, and they need to ensure that they are making regular payments against that debt to keep from becoming too highly leveraged in their tech stack. The purpose of this book is to help executives from all disciplines understand the impact of high enterprise tech debt to their operations, and to help establish a common vernacular for addressing, measuring, and managing that tech debt so that the appropriate tech debt payments can be made over time.

The Burden of Enterprise Tech Debt

As we embark on this exploration of enterprise tech debt, it is important to note that it is not merely a technical issue but a pervasive business concern. Tech debt is a burden that weighs heavily on organizations, often hidden in plain sight but affecting their financial health, operational efficiency, customer satisfaction, and their ability to innovate and thrive. This is evidenced in the Southwest and Equifax examples.

Digital transformation efforts often struggle and frequently are abandoned because of high enterprise tech debt and the challenges that arise in trying to address and reduce the tech debt leverage within the company. In the chapters ahead I will share specific examples from my over 20 years in the CIO seat that highlight this truth. I will explain how the ability to measure and manage tech debt would have helped right the ship had the discussion of tech debt leverage been part of the executive team culture in those organizations. I will also attempt to unravel the complexity of enterprise tech debt, exploring its various forms and consequences. Using real-world examples of organizations that grappled with tech debt's hidden costs I will present strategies and solutions for measuring, managing, and mitigating this debt effectively. My goal is to empower leaders with the knowledge and tools necessary to navigate the challenges of enterprise tech debt, ultimately ensuring that technology remains an enabler rather than a hindrance to their organizations' success.

Every Company Is Now a Technology Company

The assertion that "every company is a technology company" has become a prevailing concept in the business world, emphasizing the pivotal role that technology plays across all industries and sectors. This statement underscores the idea that technology is no longer merely a support function but a core driver of business success. Here are just a few reasons why this concept is so closely tied to having a clear understanding of enterprise tech debt leverage:

1. **Digital Transformation is Pervasive**: In today's business landscape, organizations in virtually every industry are undergoing some form of digital transformation. They are adopting digital technologies to improve processes, enhance customer experiences, and gain a competitive edge. As technology becomes intertwined with business operations, the management of tech debt becomes critical to ensure that digital initiatives remain effective and sustainable. Understanding the concept of enterprise tech debt drives the discussions around adoption of technology, connectivity with existing data sets, and integration with current workflows. Without a clear understanding of enterprise tech debt leverage, transformational activities cannot be accurately estimated and planned.

2. **Customer Expectations are Tech-Driven**: Customers, regardless of the industry, now have elevated expectations for seamless digital experiences. Whether it's in retail, healthcare, finance, or manufacturing, customers expect user-friendly interfaces, mobile apps, online services, and real-time information access. Tech debt can hinder an organization's ability to meet these expectations, leading to customer dissatisfaction.

3. **Data-Driven Decision-Making is Business Critical**: Data is a valuable asset for companies across the board. Good data, modeled well and appropriately interpreted, informs decision-making, enables personalized marketing, and enhances operational efficiency. Tech debt can compromise data quality, data security, and data accessibility, undermining the organization's ability to leverage those data for strategic purposes. Data itself can add to the amount of enterprise tech debt leverage within an organization, and, as we will see, too much data can create liabilities and friction points that inhibit progress rather than drive it.

4. **Operational Efficiency and Innovation are Differentiators**: Modern businesses rely on technology to streamline operations and drive innovation. Whether it's automating routine tasks, optimizing supply chains, or developing new products and services, tech debt can hinder these efforts by slowing down IT systems and increasing the cost of maintenance. High tech debt leverage can make it much more challenging to digitize workflows and to automate rote tasks. Things that should be simple to automate become challenging and extend the time to completion for these key transformational activities.

5. **The Competitive Landscape is Rapidly Shifting in all Verticals**: In a world where disruption is commonplace, organizations must remain agile and adaptable. Tech

debt can be a significant impediment to agility, making it challenging for companies to pivot, respond to market changes, or embrace emerging technologies that could disrupt their industries. CEOs and other line-of-business execs get frustrated when they are unable to move quickly to capture market share, or when they lag behind their more agile competitors. High tech debt leverage inhibits the ability to pivot because the workflows, data, or processes are built into the old systems, thus making it considerably more challenging to adapt to new methodologies or implement new workflows.

6. **Security and Compliance are Growing Concerns Across all Industries**: Cybersecurity and regulatory compliance are paramount concerns for all companies. No company wants to be on the front page with a breach announcement, yet we continue to see more companies announcing data breaches and cybersecurity events. These events erode confidence in the brand, and customers are not quick to forgive when their private data is lost. Tech debt, especially in terms of outdated software or infrastructure, can introduce vulnerabilities and compliance risks that can have severe financial and reputational consequences.

7. **Scalability and Growth Require Technology Enablement**: Companies aspire to scale their operations and expand into new markets. Agility is key. Being first to market with a new product or even a new process

(i.e., workflow) can have a significant market advantage. Enterprise tech debt can limit scalability, making it difficult to upgrade, update, or expand infrastructure, integrate new technologies, or scale in support of a growing user base.

8. **Cost Management is Key**: Managing costs is an ongoing concern for all businesses. Margins decrease, and reliance on current technology becomes key to operational efficiencies. Speed becomes a critical business capability. High enterprise tech debt leverage can lead to higher operational costs due to increased maintenance efforts, inefficient processes, and the need for emergency fixes. It can redirect human resources to maintenance and IT firefighting and away from development of new competitive capabilities.

Given these considerations, a clear understanding of enterprise tech debt is crucial for every company, regardless of its industry. It helps organizations identify and mitigate the hidden risks and costs associated with outdated or poorly maintained technology. By proactively addressing tech debt, companies can better position themselves for success in the digital age, ensuring that technology remains an enabler rather than an obstacle to achieving their strategic goals.

Chapter 2

PERNICIOUS PROBLEMS
OF TECH DEBT

The Effect of CIO Tenure on Tech Debt

The CIO is at the forefront of managing tech debt within an organization. They play a critical role in making decisions regarding IT investments, technology selection, and strategic planning. A seasoned CIO can create a roadmap for addressing tech debt, prioritizing initiatives, and ensuring that IT resources are allocated effectively. This is no easy balance, as the CEO wants to grow the top line, the CFO wants cost containment, the product, sales, and marketing folks want new capabilities for customers, and all executives want improved workflows to make their employees more efficient. As these various priorities are discussed at the executive level, the CIO has to drive the conversation around prioritization. What is most important? Here are just a few of the activities that often compete for the same resources within a company when attempting to make these prioritization decisions:

1. Patch critical systems to protect against the latest vulner-
    abilities in an effort to guard sensitive data and mitigate
    the possibility of a breach.

2. Upgrade or replace old servers and operating systems to
    increase capacity and performance to the sales systems.

3. Build new capabilities in the form of workflows and the
    accompanying data models for a new sales and market-
    ing initiative that is planned for two months from now.

4. Respond to the alerts for broken data pipelines that
    supply the daily/weekly executive reports that show how
    the business is operating.

5. Respond to an outage from a business-critical vendor
    that is currently preventing the online sales system from
    processing customer payments.

The list can go on and on. When the CIO asks the executive
team which of these is top priority, the answer is typically "all of
them." And new initiatives are added regularly, without taking
other things off the plate.

I was once involved in the executive meetings of a company
where the revenues were declining significantly and layoffs were
planned. We had also been working on several initiatives to grow
revenues, but these hadn't borne any fruit yet. As we sat in these
meetings, I had to report out on the cuts I was making to meet

the reduction plans and on our progress toward completing these revenue-generating activities at the same time. These were obviously conflicting priorities, but when I asked which initiatives we were deprioritizing as the company reduced in size, no one could agree on which initiatives could be delayed. We needed the additional revenue from these new activities, but the budget was reducing and could not support the investment. We had to cut employees, yet we were still expected to provide the new capabilities in the system so that we could avoid another layoff next quarter. It was a never-ending downward spiral. Adding to the challenges was the fact that in this particular company we had an extremely high tech debt leverage that had been built up over many years of de-prioritizing IT maintenance activities in favor of theoretical business growth initiatives that never achieved their business goals. In these situations, the CIO and their IT department is often seen as the failure point; however, the real failure point is the time and effort required to make tech debt payments while new revenue opportunities pass by without the resources to apply to them.

Another major headwind for CIOs and their IT departments is the fact that IT initiatives take time to produce meaningful results for their business, and the effects of various decisions regarding the IT stack have a longer tail than what is typically experienced in other departments. For example, when a company decides to either increase or decrease spending in a specific marketing channel, the results of that decision can often be seen in very short order—in weeks or months. When making a change in the tech stack, however, it could easily take many months before the effects are recognized in the business KPIs. This creates a very challenging environment in which CIOs must operate.

The same challenges apply to changes in personnel as well as changes in the tech stack. This problem materializes in the form of the "five-year CIO lifecycle." Year One is typically described as the honeymoon phase, where executives are excited with the "new vision" that the new CIO brings to the organization and the challenges and issues of the prior IT leadership are exposed. Year Two is spent building the new strategy and creating the new IT vision. Year Three is when the rubber really hits the road while the new strategy starts to get into place. By Year Four the timelines are being investigated more closely and the CIO is falling out of favor with the rest of the executive team. By Year Five the CIO transition is underway (again). This is a typical cycle for a CIO within a company, often with even more compressed timelines. As I am writing this chapter, I have learned of two CIOs of fairly large national retail organizations who have been dismissed from their roles after less than 12 months. I have also been made aware of two financial services institutions that have let their CIOs go after less than 24 months. In all of these cases, the IT teams indicated that these CIOs were some of the best their company has ever seen, and the IT teams felt that these leaders were making significant strides in improving the tech stack, building strong collaborative cultures, and making positive work environments for their teams. Yet the CEOs didn't feel that their CIO was getting the job done, and they initiated a change for the role.

The CIO cannot execute strategic plans if they are not around long enough to see them through. **Tech debt reduction requires prioritization of tech debt payments while simultaneously building new capabilities for business growth.** This takes significant investments in time and effort within an organization, and more often than not require the same resources that are needed for implementing new solutions. CIOs find themselves portrayed as obstructionists rather than enablers of the business. The irony of this categorization is that the tech debt is the obstruction, not the CIO. And the tech debt has likely accumulated as the result of business decisions being made without regard to tech debt payments.

I once worked for a CFO whose favorite phrase was to "kick the can" whenever it came to tech debt payments. There was always something else to spend money on, and the tech debt payments were never the highest priority for their business. Yet the tech debt within that company was holding them back. Each time they kicked the can down the road they were increasing their tech debt because they would add some new technology or capability on top of the struggling foundation. The new tech took more back-end, unseen work to maintain and to keep it running. Most CIOs are simply trying to reduce the tech debt so the company can move faster toward their strategic goals, yet they are seen as getting in the way and slowing down progress of new initiatives.

Because of this, the average tenure of a CIO stands at around four years.[4] CIO turnover poses a significant challenge when it comes to addressing tech debt, and this becomes a negative cycle in many organizations. CEOs replace their CIO because they aren't progressing the business goals, yet the very act of replacing the CIO reduces their ability to progress. This is because they are addressing what they *perceive* to be the cause, but in reality is only a *symptom* of the root cause: enterprise tech debt. Short tenures also limit that CIO's ability to initiate and oversee long-term tech debt reduction strategies effectively. It takes time for a new CIO to get up to speed, recognize the tech debt leverage, and create a new plan for prioritizing those tech debt payments.

This short CIO tenure causes many problems for organizations rather than helping them. Here are just a few of the challenges specifically relating to tech debt that are compounded by frequently changing the IT leadership within a company:

- **Disrupted Continuity**: When a CIO departs, they often take with them institutional knowledge about the organization's tech debt landscape and strategies for managing it. New CIOs must start from scratch, leading to potential disruption in ongoing efforts.

- **IT Employee Turnover**: When leaders leave, employees often do as well (whether they're loyal to that leader and follow them out the door or are so frustrated by the changes that they abandon ship). That turnover equates to lost institutional knowledge, lowered morale, project risk, etc.

- **Inconsistent Prioritization**: With each new CIO, priorities can shift and the focus on tech debt may wane. This inconsistency in prioritization can lead to delayed or abandoned efforts to address tech debt, perpetuating the problem.

- **Increased Risk**: Inconsistent management of tech debt increases the risk of system failures, security breaches, and operational inefficiencies. These risks can be costly in both financial and reputational terms.

- **Higher Costs**: With frequent turnover, an organization may invest in projects or systems that do not align with a long-term strategy for tech debt reduction. These misaligned investments result in higher costs over time.

- **Reduced Employee Morale**: Employees tasked with managing and mitigating tech debt may become frustrated and demoralized as they witness their efforts repeatedly disrupted by changes in leadership.

The average four-year tenure of a CIO may seem like a typical aspect of corporate leadership, but it has far-reaching implications for an organization's tech debt. Tech debt is a long-term problem that requires consistent attention and strategic planning. Frequent CIO turnover disrupts continuity, leads to inconsistent prioritization, and increases risk and costs. To ensure a healthier digital future, organizations must implement strategies that transcend leadership changes and prioritize the effective management of tech debt as a strategic imperative. Only then can they navigate the ever-evolving tech landscape with confidence and resilience.

I recently had lunch with a colleague who has worked in IT in their company for 20 years. They have seen four CIOs in the last *four years*. The most recent one was, in his opinion, making the most progress yet in modernizing their infrastructure and retiring tech debt. That CIO had just been let go two days prior to our conversation, after only 10 months on the job. Obviously, the executive team, or at least the CEO, saw this CIO's accomplishments vastly differently than the IT organization saw them. This is not an isolated incident. The disparity between how a CIO is performing with regard to solving their core problems within a company's tech stack and the way they are perceived by other executives is a significant problem within many companies today. Turnover at the IT executive level provides air cover for poor leadership above. It allows the CEO or COO to use the excuse that the dust is still settling due to the org change to buy 12+ months for not meeting overall business goals. The CIO becomes the scapegoat, while tech debt remains unaddressed and the business remains at risk

IT Is the Business

Another common problem is the idea that somehow there is a distinction between IT and "the business." Viewing IT as separate from "the business" is nothing more than veiled villain/victim thinking, and simply drives wedges between departments. This can have disastrous effects on the overall health of the business. Feeding the thought process that IT is separate and distinct from the business can lead to significantly increased enterprise tech debt. This can show up in the form of siloed decision-making, lack of overall strategic alignment, and failure to align on prioritization of tech debt payments.

Siloed decision-making will show up in the form of business leaders making decisions without fully understanding the technological implications, and IT decisions not aligning with broader business goals. This type of siloed decision-making can result in the accumulation of tech debt as business leaders may prioritize short-term gains, ignoring the long-term sustainability of technology solutions. This can lead to the adoption of quick fixes, outdated systems, and architectural decisions that favor expediency over robustness. This leaves poorly planned solutions as the back-office engine for new initiatives, often leaving a significant gap between expectations and reality as the new solutions are cobbled together with legacy systems.

These opposing forces from differing departmental silos lead to a clear lack of strategic alignment between IT and "the business." Line of business leaders who do not include IT in their planning (because they don't see IT as partners in running their business) make decisions that are not aligned with the technological strategic roadmap. The IT projects that do make it into the strategic roadmap are often not aligned with the needs of the rest of the departments because IT is unaware of those needs.

When IT projects are not aligned with business goals, they may be more likely to become technical liabilities, and thus contribute to tech debt rather than reduce it. These projects may also lack the support and funding needed for ongoing maintenance and upgrades, leading to additional tech debt accumulation. This type of siloed environment can also lead to direct hard costs from the accumulation of tech debt.

I once worked for a company where the CEO had given department heads significant autonomy. As a result we had substantial duplication of services across the company. It eventually came to my attention that one of the other departments was interviewing vendors for a specific capability that we already had within our environment. In fact, we already had contracts with three competing vendors to provide this capability, and our IT roadmap aimed to consolidate these down to a single vendor over the next 12 months. When I became aware that this department was investigating yet another vendor, I brought them into our steering committee to discuss their needs and try to gain alignment with our strategic IT roadmap. Our CFO was one of the attendees of the steering committee. As part of the discussion, the marketing department indicated that this particular solution would only cost $50,000 per year, and they had the funds within their budget to cover this expense (even though it would actually come out of my budget).

I countered that the cost would invariably rise with more use, and that the $50,000 was immediately considered tech debt since we were planning to consolidate all of these duplicative systems into one. Our recommendation was to use the proposed funds to help speed up the consolidation effort and provide the needed capabilities for everyone rather than spending the funds to add a fourth duplicate system into our tech stack just for their department.

The CFO ultimately decided that $50,000 was not a large investment, and since marketing had the budget they were allowed to proceed. A short 18 months later this product was costing the company $320,000 a year, and we had only retired two of the duplicative systems. By this time the marketing department was complaining that they could not support the provisioning, maintenance, and upkeep of this solution and they were asking to move it into the IT department's budget and support infrastructure.

In addition to the hard costs associated with these types of siloed decisions, mis-aligned strategic initiatives can also lead to communication gaps between technical teams and their line-of-business counterparts. In the example above, the system in question became a huge lightening rod and caused rifts between IT and marketing that have yet to be repaired. Misunderstandings and miscommunications occur, making it challenging to convey the technical aspects of tech debt to those lines of business. Effective communication between departments is essential for addressing tech debt. When there are communication gaps, tech debt issues may go unnoticed or unaddressed, and thus may establish roadblocks for the lines of business to reach their business goals. Developers and other IT technologists may struggle to convey the importance of addressing tech debt, leading to a lack of support from non-technical stakeholders. Without a proper understanding of the ways in which the tech debt is hampering the achievement of business goals, there will be a tendency to prioritize new projects and features over addressing tech debt. The focus may be on delivering visible results to the detriment of maintaining and improving existing systems. Neglecting tech debt in favor of new projects will lead to its accumulation. Over time, this can result in outdated systems, inefficient processes, and increased maintenance costs. The organization may struggle to innovate or adapt to changing market conditions due to the burden of tech debt.

Keeping IT at arm's length from the rest of the business increases tech debt within the organization as a whole. This has been a perennial problem in IT, and one that I have seen at almost every company where I have worked throughout my 30+ year career. IT folks become "ticket takers," simply trying to accommodate "the business" by doing exactly what they are asked to do. They know that there may be a better way to accomplish the business goal, but they are not consulted until a technical direction has already been determined. So they try to make it work, often by cobbling together solutions that otherwise could have been much more efficiently designed.

My mantra for highlighting this problem and attempting to mitigate it is this: **give IT a problem to solve, not a solution to implement**. I have frequently offered this advice to my peers as we strive to build better relationships between IT and the rest of the business. Bring IT folks to the table to help solve problems, and you will end up with better solutions in the end.

I recently spoke to two peer CIOs, each with a vastly different story to tell me. The primary reason for the different stories and outcomes was the relationship between IT and the rest of the business. In one instance, the IT department came to the table to discuss, negotiate, and drive direction relating to a time-sensitive opportunity that meant 50% improvement in their overall business. Despite challenges, difficulties, and many missteps, this company successfully accomplished their next-to-impossible feat (all completed this calendar year) and are well on their way to meeting their overall goals for this initiative.

The other instance is an all-too-common tale. The IT team was tasked with delivering a transformative initiative—and left alone to complete it. This was a huge, multi-year initiative, and everyone knew that the future of the company was dependent on its success. The goal was a completely new platform upon which the company would run their core business, thus allowing them to scale up. While IT was busy working on this, the rest of the business left them alone, but still had needs within their departments. They found and implemented various new point solutions and struggled to integrate their data with other departments. Because they didn't want to "bother" IT, they researched solutions and vendors on their own and found cloud solutions that (according to the vendor) didn't require IT help to implement. Of course, they eventually ran into challenges as they attempted to connect their data, and then had to reach out to IT to establish the connection. By this time, it was obviously far too late for IT to help find a better way to solve these one-off problems in ways that aligned with the new platform, so they had to take time away from their transformation work to help fix the problems with each of these point solutions.

Needless to say, the "transformation" was eventually deemed a failure and the entire initiative was scrapped—all at a huge sunk cost to the company on top of the lost opportunity cost of not having a new platform after years of work.

What was the difference? In the first instance, IT was seen as a critical partner in solving the problem, and they helped come up with the plan in the first place. In the second, the IT team was seen as nothing more than the implementation team, and they were left out of the solutioning and problem solving, especially as related to the point solutions. All of the solutioning was left to the business experts.

It is never too early to loop in IT. Companies that collaborate with IT to find solutions as soon as they identify a problem, begin defining a new product, uncover a new need, or start any initiative have significantly better success managing their tech debt and meeting their overall business goals. Using true agile principles to engage all experts and to deliver incrementally and consistently will help remove the silos and reduce your overall tech debt. Bringing IT to the table to help solve business problems is one way to make significant tech debt payments and reduce your tech debt leverage while making progress toward strategic business goals.

Companies that don't get this right suffer the consequences. Digital transformation spending, which includes data analytics and digital technology, was estimated to be about $2 trillion globally in 2023 and is expected to reach $3.4 trillion by 2026. Yet most CEOs are not seeing the value from this spend reflected in improvements to their business operations. Why? Tech debt.

As reported in a recent *Wall Street Journal* article, "Few companies have the aptitude and enthusiasm to adapt, integrate and improve upon technology investments with each iteration... Having the right leadership team is essential, as is a clear road map. Without that capacity, companies struggle to drive productivity from technology."[5] This is a direct reflection of the challenge of leaving the CIO and the IT team out of the strategic business initiative discussions and allowing companies to operate IT and "the business" as separate and distinct operations.

Every company is now a technology company, but many are not yet acting like technology companies. Everyone knows how to gather data, but very few know how to extract value by turning that data into actionable information. One of the key statistics that I referenced in my doctoral study is the fact that companies today are effectively utilizing less than 5% of their available data for making key business decisions. They spend incredible amounts of money to gather, store, and analyze those data, and they talk about all of the data they have collected—they just don't turn it into information that can be acted upon.

Transforming a company to a true digital organization that effectively utilizes data for decision-making takes the entire company thinking differently than it has in the past. It requires knowledge, skillset, and expertise within the company leadership around data architecture and data analysis that has not existed in most companies before. Too often the CIO and the IT team are seen as infrastructure and support rather than as key members of the digital transformation team.

This change requires a data-driven CIO and an IT team that is fully engaged with their business. Every great tech company had both a radical innovator and a rational innovator at the helm. The radical innovator identifies the mountain that their company needs to climb, while the rational innovator identifies what roads, bridges, and paths need to be built to make it to the top of that mountain. Some examples of radical innovators / rational inno-vators include Steve Jobs / Steve Wozniack (Apple) and Bill Gates / Steve Balmer (Microsoft). When it comes to digital transforma-tions and data-driven companies, the CEO can be considered the radical innovator, and the CIO would be the rational innovator. Both are required for a successful transformation.

Viewing IT as separate from "the business" can create a disconnect that has detrimental effects on tech debt. Siloed decision-making, a lack of strategic alignment, communication gaps, failure to prioritize tech debt, risk aversion, and missed opportunities for innovation all contribute to the accumulation of tech debt. **To effectively manage and reduce tech debt, organizations must bridge the gap between IT and the broader business, ensuring that technology decisions align with strategic objectives and that tech debt is recognized and addressed as a shared responsibility.**

In this chapter, we've explored the multifaceted nature of enterprise tech debt, recognizing that it extends well beyond traditional software development concerns. It encompasses an array of challenges, from architecture and vendor dependencies to security and compliance. The ripples of tech debt touch every facet of an organization, affecting its operations, innovation, risk profile, and agility.

In the chapters ahead, we will delve deeper into the consequences of enterprise tech debt and explore strategies for identifying, quantifying, and addressing it effectively. The journey continues as we equip leaders with the knowledge and tools to navigate the complexities of tech debt in the modern digital landscape.

Chapter 3

THE HIDDEN COSTS OF ENTERPRISE TECH DEBT

The Deceptive Nature of Hidden Costs

Hidden costs are the silent adversaries of enterprise tech debt. They are the expenses, risks, and consequences that lurk beneath the surface, gradually accumulating like a submerged iceberg, until their impact becomes undeniable. In this chapter, we will illuminate the depths of these hidden costs, shedding light on their diverse forms and the profound implications they carry.

IT Projects Are Never Done

One of the key contributors to tech debt is the concept of IT projects and the assumptions around how we manage them. Tech debt accumulates as IT projects roll off the finish line and the company (theoretically) reassigns those IT resources to a new project or initiative. Anyone who has worked in IT knows that this is never a clean break, and all IT projects and initiatives need ongoing care and feeding to keep them operating efficiently. Ignoring that care and feeding leads to the accumulation of tech debt.

We need a better way of collaborating between IT and the rest of the business. One of the biggest problems, in my opinion, is how we talk about IT projects, and how non-IT folks perceive the creative process associated with building technological solutions. One of the worst things to happen to the field of IT was when someone decided to use the analogy of construction projects to describe the creative process surrounding technological solutions.

While the construction analogy has its merits, as it helps us understand key concepts such as architecture, design, and operational project management, it also significantly contributes to the accumulation of tech debt within an organization. This is because the construction analogy implies that IT projects have an endpoint, much like construction of a building. When the building is complete, the construction crew hands it over to whomever is going to own and occupy the building, and they move on to their next construction project. This is not the reality for IT projects, and it is a significant downside of using this ubiquitous analogy to describe how IT and the rest of the business should interact.

Construction projects, whether it's building a skyscraper or a bridge, have a clear endpoint. Once the project is complete, the construction team can move on to their next endeavor, giving it their undivided attention. The structure stands independently, requiring minimal maintenance beyond occasional repairs or renovations.

In contrast, IT projects, once completed, don't enjoy the luxury of a clear endpoint. They demand ongoing care and attention, akin to tending to a golf course. The process of designing, architecting, and building a new hole on the golf course mirrors that of IT projects. Once completed, this new hole isn't left to its own devices; it requires ongoing maintenance, including mowing, trimming, watering, and care to ensure it remains in optimal condition. Likewise, data must be monitored, software patched, and security vulnerabilities addressed regularly to keep the system current and secure.

This crucial distinction between construction and IT projects lies at the heart of understanding the unique challenges posed by enterprise tech debt. This analogy provides a much better perspective on IT projects and tech debt within enterprises. Just as a golf course must continuously invest in maintaining its holes, so must organizations invest in the maintenance and improvement of their IT systems. Ignoring this aspect can lead to the accumulation of tech debt, where outdated software, unpatched vulnerabilities, and inefficient processes hinder the organization's ability to achieve its goals.

The parallel between golf course maintenance and IT system care offers a valuable lesson in managing and limiting tech debt. Just as a golf course owner wouldn't neglect their greens and fairways, enterprise leaders should prioritize the care and feeding of their IT systems. This includes regular updates, security measures, and improvements to ensure that the technology landscape remains relevant and supports the company's evolving needs. Most companies don't have the luxury of creating independent maintenance teams who care for their released systems. This is one of the significant contributors to tech debt over time.

In summary, while the construction project analogy has its merits in understanding IT initiatives, it falls short in capturing the ongoing care and maintenance required by IT systems. Shifting our perspective to that of a golf course, where new additions demand continual attention, offers a more accurate portrayal of IT projects. Recognizing the importance of the care and feeding of enterprise IT systems is essential in managing and limiting tech debt, ensuring that the technological landscape remains an asset rather than a burden. By adopting this mindset, CIOs, CEOs, CFOs, and board members can navigate the complex terrain of enterprise tech debt and make informed decisions to propel their organizations forward.

Tech Debt and Systemic Risk

As discussed in the introduction of this book, the term "tech debt" was originally coined by one of the signers of the Agile Manifesto as a way to define custom software development shortcuts that inhibit functionality later in the product lifecycle. In recent years it has become more generally accepted to refer to any technological issue that is holding back your ability to deliver on company goals. The former is almost solely a derogatory term (reflecting laziness or bad decisions), whereas the latter is simply a recognition of the reality of the rapid rate of change in technology that is extremely challenging to keep up with while still advancing your corporate strategy. In this chapter we address the benefits of using the broader definition of tech debt and why it is important for companies to measure and manage their tech debt leverage as a way to combat enterprise systemic risk.

Using the broader definition of tech debt provides a way for executive teams to have a conversation around the relationship between tech debt and systemic risk. The concept of systemic risk entered common vernacular during the financial crisis of 2008 and was initially focused primarily on the global financial system. Systemic risk refers to the potential for a failure or crisis in one or more parts of the financial system to spread and cause extensive disruption to the entire system. The term is easily applied to enterprise IT systems, especially from the perspectives of cybersecurity and tech debt.

We are currently witnessing a significant shift as boardrooms are being forced to address systemic risk. The recent changes announced by the SEC[6] regarding cybersecurity expertise on boards is part of that shift, and boards and executive teams are being tasked with directly addressing systemic risk within their organizations. Accountability is being demanded where it hasn't been before. Systemic risk is one of the biggest challenges facing most organizations today, and tech debt is one of the primary drivers of systemic risk. Yet most executive teams don't pay attention to either one.

A couple of real-world examples may help to make this point.

I was once brought in to help a company that had started their digital transformation but had made several key mistakes launching their modernization effort. By the time they brought me in they were two years and $10 million into their transformation, yet they had nothing actually running in any production systems on their new platform. They had taken a "build it and they will come" approach, which really means they were forcing themselves into a "big bang" rollout. For key enterprise systems, the big bang approach almost always fails.

The IT department was unable to deliver because their new solution was never good enough to fully replace existing workflows. Consultants and contractors had been hired to build the new system, while the internal IT team was left to maintain the existing system while the new one was being developed. This only magnified the problems because while the new platform was being built the old platform was still evolving, as the internal IT team was constantly maintaining and adding new features. But because they knew that the replacement solution was "almost done" they cut corners constantly when maintaining the old system and only did the bare minimum to get the new capabilities working. They consciously overlooked some issues in the code because they felt it would be a waste of time to fix it since the new platform was going to replace the old system "very soon."

It was a never-ending downward spiral; the business kept asking for changes, IT delivered those changes by consciously cutting corners for faster delivery, and the outsourced contractors working on the new platform couldn't keep up with the new features while maintaining progress on the new platform functionality. As a result, the business felt less and less confident in the new platform. Why would they need it? The old one was working just fine, and in some ways the old system was already better than the new one because of the new workflows being implemented. They had no idea that it was running on unpatched servers that were over a decade behind and using code libraries that were four major revisions behind. Tech debt was accumulating at an accelerated rate. The more the code was updated, the farther behind it became, and the less demand there was from the business to migrate to the new system.

They were now in a very tough situation because stabilizing their old platform was going to be very expensive and time-consuming, but the new platform wasn't yet ready to take on any production workflows. To make matters worse, their top line revenue was diminishing quickly due to a perfect storm of business factors, including global macroeconomic post-pandemic conditions and poor executive decisions that led to regulatory scrutiny related to their core business. To say that it was a very challenging time for this company would be a significant understatement.

As I joined the company we made some immediate changes in the approach to the new platform. We brought the development in-house and focused on releasing the capabilities that had already been developed. At first, we made significant progress in standing up the new platform and building out the functionality to accept production workflows. We connected the data pipelines and replaced key workflows as we introduced the new platform to the lines of business. But the progress wasn't fast enough, as the revenues dropped off faster than anyone had predicted. The business could no longer sustain the cost of maintaining both production platforms, and we arrived at a key inflection point; we needed to either go all-in on the new platform or we needed to halt the transformation and revert back to the old system completely. But we now had a foot on both sides of the fence; there were active production workflows running through both systems, so either way would mean some immediate and significant changes to someone's business processes. The hard costs were approximately the same for either solution, as migrating to the new platform would remove around $5 million in duplicative capabilities from old systems, and removing the new platform would have a similar effect on the budget, not counting the sunk cost of the implementation to date.

Either way it was a tough decision, but when I laid out the options for the CEO and CFO my strong recommendation was to continue the transformation. Retire the tech debt, accelerate the move to the new platform, and remove the duplication across the enterprise by moving workflows into the new platform and retiring old systems faster than initially planned. This path would significantly reduce their tech debt and set them up for success in their digital transformation despite the diminishing revenues and pressure on the core business. They were unconvinced and decided to take the more comfortable path of sticking with their old, comfortable systems. They decided to "kick the can" (a direct quote from the CEO) and kill the transformation, which meant directing the IT team to put significant focus on the outdated systems by updating on-premise server operating systems, upgrading development libraries, and re-building workflow capabilities in the old platform for all of the workflows that had been transitioned to the new platform. Their decision meant remaining on their old, comfortable platform that had driven their success for the past 20 years—and a significant increase in their tech debt leverage rather than reducing it in favor of modernized systems.

This decision also carried with it significantly more systemic risk than the alternative. Looking in from the outside one may wonder how such a decision would be made and may think that this was a unique business in an uncommon situation faced with an impossible choice. But as this was unfolding, I had lunch with a friend who explained how a very similar situation was currently unfolding at his company. His CEO had also recently decided to throw in the towel on their transformation, and they were actively reverting to their comfortable, old, (arguably) reliable platform. The way he expressed it was that his CEO saw their engine cranking out cash and all he wanted the IT team to do was to keep that engine running, even though that engine was old, failing, and (mostly) unstable. When faced with the prospect of building a new engine, and more specifically when he saw the investment needed to do so, the CEO was unconvinced that the new engine was needed. Just keep the current engine running and don't waste any time or money trying to build something new.

Another example occurred when I was asked to help a company through a merger. I was asked to help evaluate the IT systems of both entities, and to opine on the ability to combine these systems in short order. These were healthcare institutions where connectivity into the Electronic Health Records (EHR) was critically important. The hardware specs aligned between the two organizations, and on paper it looked like a fairly good match. Theoretically the new EHR would be able to operate on the acquired company's hardware, and the transition would be smooth. As I took a closer look at the actual hardware, however, it became very clear to me that the systems were in a significant state of disrepair. The acquired company had known for some time that they were shopping themselves around, and they had stopped spending money on the maintenance of their hardware. My recommendation was for the acquiring company to replace all of the hardware as part of the merger. The CEO was not pleased with the projected costs associated with this proposal and decided that this was not a requirement for the merger. We proceeded with their existing hardware and attempted to operate without updating it. Within two months of the acquisition, the systems began failing and we ended up having to reallocate funds to replace them anyway. But now we had to do it reactively and without having budgeted for the expense. This resolution also came with much more operational impact than it would have had if we had planned the replacements and completed them as part of the merger plan. This was an example of pure systemic risk due to manageable tech debt that could have been proactively retired but instead turned into a reactive emergency for IT and a disaster for operations. The reputational damage was also severe as the employees lost confidence in the acquiring entity and their management team.

These examples all demonstrate the real-world operational challenges that arise from failing to manage tech debt and highlight the systemic risk that grows out of this mismanagement. This is the significant challenge that tech debt brings to an organization. It hides in the background, often under the guise of "working systems." The byproduct of tech debt is systemic risk, as old platforms are harder to patch, leaving security vulnerabilities exposed. These aging platforms also carry with them the risk of failing due to aging infrastructure and unreliable hardware, and even more importantly they have the risk of being unable to support new workflows due to poor data structures and limited connectivity options for new data pipelines. So the systemic risk builds quietly, behind the scenes, while businesses function seemingly smoothly. Unless the CEO can understand the impact of that tech debt and the systemic risk that it poses to the core engine of the business, they are not going to be willing to provide the funding or the organizational support to resolve it, and systemic risk will continue to build up undetected.

While the traditional definition of tech debt is limited to custom software development, the broader definition allows for discussions around systemic risk built up within an organization due to decisions around their enterprise platform. It is only by quantifying the tech debt that you can associate it with systemic risk; then, you can have a basis for discussion with the executive team around risk reduction by managing tech debt. Without quantifying tech debt, business decisions will be made based on the old, comfortable, current status quo. And systemic risk will increase.

Chapter 4

DATA AS TECH DEBT

It has been said that data is the new gold, or more appropriately that data is the new soil from which all things will grow. A study of corporate investment in data assets spanning the 20-year period starting in 2002 indicated that the cumulative nominal investment in data was $2.6 trillion, and internal investment in data assets grew from $84 billion at the start to $186 billion at the end of that 20-year period.[7]

Extracting value from those data has been a significant challenge to companies, especially as organizations try to adapt to the challenge of transitioning from traditional data analytics to big data analysis, which was the focus of my 2020 doctoral study.[8]

The issues associated with enterprise tech debt as discussed in this book are also quite applicable to data storage within organizations, for many of the same reasons that tech debt applies to enterprise systems. Companies hoard data with the idea that they might possibly someday maybe need some insights that may only be gained by evaluating historical data that they might as well store today. This flawed logic leads to tech debt in many forms, and often hampers the very efforts that the thinking was intended to support in the first place.

I once worked with a marketing team who was attempting to access the vast amount of customer data stored in their proprietary customer relation management solution. They had over 20 years of customer data stored in this system, and their business offering was one that customers could utilize multiple times throughout their life. Remarketing to previous customers was a critical path to success, but in order to do this right they needed a new marketing communications solution. They invested in Salesforce Marketing Cloud in an attempt to modernize their systems and mine the value out of their vast storage of customer data.

They quickly ran into problems as they attempted to access this valuable data. They were unwilling to put in the time to properly connect the new Salesforce system with their legacy proprietary solution. Instead, they created a complex set of ETL processes to extract the data elements from the legacy system and load them into the new Salesforce solution. They quickly realized that the data in their legacy system was not clean or well maintained, and they were unable to clearly identify any specific customer data set as they transitioned it into the new environment.

The fact that they had hoarded all of this customer data was of little value in the end. In fact, it became a deterrent to their ability to implement the new marketing communications strategy because not only were they unwilling to make a clean break with their old data, they were also unwilling to make the investment to clean it up so it would become usable. Instead, they spent quite a bit of time and money trying to fix and stabilize their ETL processes as a Band-Aid solution to their data woes. They never were able to fully realize their remarketing vision because their old data was holding them back. It was **data as tech debt**, preventing them from moving their business forward.

This chapter addresses those various forms of tech debt that arise when companies are focused on storing data and not on maintaining, cleaning, and pruning those data along the way.

Data Generation's Exponential Growth

As I articulate in my doctoral study[9], data generation has increased exponentially in recent years, with no signs of this trend stopping. It has been estimated that globally we are generating around 2.5 exabytes of new data per day, and the Government Accountability Office has estimated that by 2025 there will be between 25 and 50 billion devices connected to the Internet and actively generating data. However, even with the vast amount of data available to them, organizations effectively use less than 5% of their available data. This stems from three potential problems for companies: they don't know how to analyze the data they have, they don't know what insights they are able to gain by analyzing the data, or they simply don't know that they have the data in the first place.

The emergence of big data has introduced even more data management challenges involving processing speed, data interpretation, and data quality for organizations that wish to consume complex information. The traditional methods, frameworks, strategies, and tools for data governance and analysis are outdated and no longer adequate for processing the vast amount of data available to organizations today, thus making current strategies ineffective for handling big data. Companies are unable to extract the value from their vast amounts of stored data because they are unable to analyze those data in a timely fashion. Big data analytics challenges arise from issues relating to data that are too vast, unstructured, and moving too fast to be managed by traditional means.

One study found that nearly 85% of Fortune 500 organizations are unable to use their data effectively. Yet companies continue to store data in the hope that one day they might be able to analyze it appropriately and somehow extract insights from the "gold mine" of data they have accumulated. In thinking this way, they disregard the fact that most data have a shelf life that will reduce its viability before the company is able to extract valuable information from it. We will investigate several reasons why this is the case in the remainder of this chapter.

Tech Debt's Effect on Decision-Making

Multiple studies have shown that the value of data is severely hampered by the lack of big data expertise within the organization. A 2017 study identified that effectively utilizing big data to make decisions poses a considerable challenge for companies. This is partially due to the fact that big data analytics rely on fuzzy logic and inductive statistics, which can lead to improper or incomplete analysis of those data, which in turn can lead to misinterpretation and ultimately result in incorrect business decisions being made from those assumptions and analysis.

Poor decision-making based on hoarded data stems from unmaintained data, rogue data, and overall poor data quality. Data hoarding only exacerbates each of these issues, as it becomes exponentially more difficult to maintain, clean, and manage data as it constantly grows within the enterprise over time. All of this becomes tech debt as companies spend time, effort, and money in a fruitless attempt to mine old data that is likely not even accurate any longer. Additionally, given the recent regulatory focus on data privacy, much of this data are not only pure tech debt but also increase liability for the company.

Tech Debt Can Significantly Affect Data Quality

An IBM survey found that poor data quality costs the US economy approximately $3.1 trillion annually,[10] and that companies are losing up to 12% of their potential revenue due to dirty, rogue (incomplete, inaccurate, irrelevant, corrupt, incorrectly formatted, or duplicative) data within their business processes. A global study[11] of 1,300 C-Suite business leaders and finance and accounting personnel found that 70% of the respondents lacked confidence in their data used for making financial decisions. Around half (56%) of the C-Suite respondents indicated that they are completely confident in the accuracy of their companies' financial data, but only 30% of the F&A professionals felt the same level of confidence. In other words, those closer to the actual data are less confident in its accuracy. As reports are generated and routed up the chain to the senior executives, those executives are more confident in the accuracy than those who performed the analysis to begin with. Consider the implications of this finding: the C-Suite executives are blissfully unaware of the data quality challenges behind the reports they receive and upon which they make critical business decisions.

This then helps to explain why 30% of business leaders in a different study report that they are not confident with the data they are using to make business decisions, and why companies today are effectively utilizing only 5% of their available data to actually make key business decisions. Companies store information with the expectation that they will return to the data when they need it. However, they do not consider the shelf life of the data they are storing, nor do they consider the data quality issues associated with those data.

Often, companies will store contact information for customers, clients, and vendors with the intent of easily contacting those individuals again in the future. However, keeping data current is a constant challenge. People change their telephone numbers (about 18% per year), they change roles within their company (about 60% per year), and CEOs move companies (about 21% per year). **Data decay is a constant challenge.** What happens when we need to access that information? Because of the lack of confidence in the data itself, it is estimated that knowledge workers spend 50% of their time wading through waste in hidden data factories, hunting for data, finding and correcting errors, and searching for confirmatory sources for data they don't trust. According to CrowdFlower, data scientists spend 60% of their time cleaning and organizing data.

This issue of analyzing rogue data is so commonly known within the data science community that it has been given a name: "the rule of ten." This rule states that it will cost 10x more for a data scientist to complete a unit of work when the data is unclean as compared to when the data is perfect.

As organizations scramble to implement artificial intelligence models, it is important to note that these AI systems are highly dependent upon data for their operations. A study by Dimensional Research found that 8 out of 10 AI / ML initiatives have stalled due to poor data quality, and 96% "have run into problems with data quality, data labeling required to train AI, and building model confidence." This is clearly data tech debt.

In another survey, "The State of Data and What's Next," 31% percent of respondents said that it's difficult to find data for their

AI models because it's constantly being moved around. Forty-three percent of respondents in another survey indicated that they use an average of four to six platforms to manage their data. Another 11% use an average of 10-12 platforms. Data sprawl is a significant contributor to technical debt within organizations, and a critical speedbump for AI initiatives.

If we aren't focusing on cleaning up our internal data, the AI models will be hampered by all of the same problems we are already facing with traditional data solutions. We won't be able to train our AI models without solving the data problems that already exist in our legacy systems and contribute to our tech debt.

Much like the deprecation to a car's value that starts as soon as you drive off the lot, the value of data starts to diminish as soon as you store it. Rogue data, data sprawl, and lack of data hygiene are severely impacting revenue opportunities within our companies. Data quality is a key aspect of tech debt.

Liability of Data Hoarding

Companies hoard data with the thought that they may want to make some analysis they haven't thought of yet to inform business decisions they haven't considered yet. As we saw in the last section, data can quickly become stale and thus lose its value for future analysis.

A common example of data hoarding is the process that most companies use regarding job seekers. Have you ever been rejected for a job, but told by the company that they will file your resume and reach out if they ever open a role where your skills better align? Companies implement applicant tracking systems (ATS) for this very purpose. They store applications, resumes, and contact information for people who have applied to roles with them. Do they ever actually use this information? In my 30 years in hiring manager roles, I have never once seen anyone actually use that data.

Worse yet, many ATSs now require that you create an account with that system before you can apply for a job. You have to create a username and password specifically for the ATS for the company at which you are applying. Job seekers are not going to create a unique password for every company to which they apply. Most will re-use the same password, thus increasing their own risk of having their password stolen because a company that never even interviewed them had a data breach and lost their data.

I have even seen some ATSs ask for personal information that would be needed if you were to accept a job there, such as a social security number, names and phone numbers of references, etc. I am sure that some HR folks felt this was a great time saver for those candidates who become employees, as they already have all of the information that they need to onboard them, but what about all of those candidates who are never interviewed, or who are interviewed and don't get hired? Data tech debt.

Considering the frequency with which this data actually gets used (or rather the lack of it), this data becomes more of a liability than an asset. Why would a company want to hold onto usernames and passwords for people they have no association with other than the fact that those people once applied to an open role? This just increases the attack surface and the number of people who will have to be informed in the case of a data breach. Why maintain all of this personal information if it is never actually going to be used? This is pure data tech debt, as it needs to be considered in business continuity / disaster recovery (BC/DR) scenarios as well as breach notification processes.

In this chapter we have discussed the various ways in which data can contribute to an organization's overall tech debt. These data challenges can lead to accumulated costs, reduced efficiency, data quality and accuracy challenges, security and compliance risks, and ineffective resource allocation.

Just as with code and technical decisions, data hoarding accumulates costs over time. When an organization stores excessive amounts of data without a clear purpose or strategy, it incurs expenses related to data storage, maintenance, and management. These costs can be substantial, particularly as data volumes grow.

Data hoarding can hinder efficiency in various ways. Retrieving relevant data from a cluttered, unorganized data repository becomes time-consuming and challenging. Employees may struggle to find the data they need when it's buried in an excess of irrelevant information, leading to productivity losses.

Data hoarding can result in lower data quality and accuracy. When data is not properly curated or updated, it becomes outdated, inconsistent, and potentially unreliable. This can lead to poor decision-making and operational inefficiencies.

As we've already discussed, storing unnecessary data can expose an organization to security and compliance risks and lead to compliance violations, especially under regulations like GDPR or CCPA.

Just as with financial debt, data hoarding ties up resources that could be better utilized elsewhere. Organizations allocate resources for storage, maintenance, and management of data that may have little or no value, diverting resources away from more strategic initiatives.

Finally, managing vast amounts of data can introduce complexity into an organization's IT infrastructure. Data hoarding may necessitate additional hardware and software solutions to handle the increased data volume, resulting in technical debt in the form of complex and difficult-to-maintain systems.

Chapter 5

TECH DEBT'S IMPACT ON INNOVATION

The accumulation of tech debt can significantly affect the ability for organizations to innovate. In a survey of over 1,000 CIOs and other tech leaders, it was reported that around 30% of IT budgets and 20% of human resources are focused on addressing tech debt within their organizations.[12] Another study reported that engineers spend 33% of their time dealing with technical debt.[13] Multiple studies estimate the average organization wastes 23%-42% of their development time on technical debt.[14] In those same studies, CIOs reported that 10%-20% of the new product technology budget is actually spent on resolving existing issues related to tech debt. A McKinsey study[15] describes one company that estimates the cost of their tech debt as anywhere between 15%-60% of every dollar spent on IT, which is not accounted for in their business cases. In that same study a large bank estimates that its 1,000 systems and applications together generate over $2 billion in tech-debt costs. Often this work done to address tech debt is not the planned activities around maintaining and reducing tech debt but rather the natural effect of unmanaged tech debt within the organization.

This strain on resources creates a significant drain on innovation, as so much of the organization is focused on maintaining and fixing rather than building.

Tech Debt Hampers Innovation

Twice in my career I have been brought into an organization that was so impaired by their forced focus on tech debt that it was having significant effects on the overall business. On both cases, their technology was holding them back in very meaningful ways, and they were completely dependent upon the people who had built that tech in the first place. They were simply trying to plug the holes in the dam and running out of ways to do it. Their tech was aging, they had no process to speak of, and they didn't know how to fix it. They had dug a hole and didn't know how to get out. They had ideas of where they wanted to innovate and move their business forward, but their legacy systems were so riddled with tech debt that their resources were hampered just trying to keep their systems running in support of their current business.

When I entered these organizations, I immediately put into effect a people, process, and then technology approach. I found that much of their problems stemmed from the fact that the people involved with architecting, designing, building, and maintaining their enterprise systems were the same people who had been doing so for 15-20 years. They were stuck because they were the experts on the legacy system and the company was heavily reliant upon these individuals because of the tribal knowledge built up within their minds. Innovation, in their mind, was whatever they had planned as the next phase of their evolution of these legacy systems. And since their data were so tightly coupled with their legacy system design, it was extremely difficult to consider alternatives that did not include these legacy systems.

In both cases, these systems were built on aging infrastructure that also had not been maintained. This simply exacerbated the problems because as these companies tried to innovate, they were hampered not only by their legacy systems, but also by their legacy infrastructure that was supporting those systems. They could not update one without updating the other, and updating everything was too disruptive to their daily operations. By their lack of focus on maintaining legacy systems and allowing their tech debt to accumulate to extreme levels, these companies had painted themselves into a corner. Since all of their valuable data were so tightly coupled and stored within these systems, they were being held hostage to their legacy systems. It was in many aspects just like watching an episode of *Hoarders*, but from the perspective of a business.

In both cases, I began by evaluating the existing staff. I found some diamonds in the rough who were in the wrong role. Once I moved them to the right one, they began to shine, and they began articulating new ideas about how to retire the tech debt. I also found some who were simply unable to change their thinking and could not separate themselves from these legacy systems into which they had put so much of their time and effort over the years. I had to make the tough decision to replace these individuals with folks who could separate themselves from the systems, and who could approach the solution from a new perspective.

Both of these organizations were already attempting to be "agile" but without any real concept of the discipline needed to do so. They both had isolated the IT function in an effort to give them the space to solve these problems, without understanding that the real solution was in better collaboration between IT and the rest of the business operations. To resolve this, we focused on the process and taught true agile principles across the entire organization. We also brought in agile experts to help lead the organization through the task of engaging those outside of the IT organization in the process.

In both cases there was a key element of tech debt that was holding us back. We addressed the tech debt, removed the logjam, and began regularly deploying working code on an agile cadence. The process took 12-18 months to complete before we were operating as an agile organization, collaborating between business entities and IT, deploying code regularly, and beginning to address the rest of the tech debt within the company. Although we were making some inroads into retiring the tech debt, it felt like we were chipping away at a mountain with a pickaxe.

In both cases, the business was being attacked by more agile competitors and very challenging global business conditions. We now had a technology strategy that would allow us to modernize and transform the foundational systems, but time was not on our side. The business didn't have enough time to address their tech debt and implement their innovative new solutions, and competitors were beginning to overtake them. The macroeconomic conditions were applying pressure to these businesses, and they were facing significant headwinds to their operations.

As the pressure built on these businesses, the executive teams began losing confidence in the modernization plan, and they began returning to their legacy thinking. They looked for ways to cobble together solutions in their legacy systems once again, and eventually both companies gave up completely on their transformation initiatives. I left shortly thereafter, and the prior tech leaders were put back in place (in both cases they had moved to other parts of the business outside of IT and now wanted to come back). They immediately made some key changes to the folks I had brought in and replaced them with the prior tech leadership that they had worked with. They focused all of their efforts on trying once again to build up their legacy systems.

In both cases, the process began to erode almost immediately and technology stack began to fall behind again. In both cases the company went out of business within a couple years. The lack of management and maintenance of tech debt inhibited their ability to innovate, hampered their ability to grow, and eventually led to each of these companies closing their doors. These are only two examples in which I had personal experience; yet this inability to innovate and grow is not limited to these two examples. It happens to many companies.

Having the right people, running the right processes, and focusing on the right technology problems by addressing tech debt is absolutely critical to the success of any company. And it starts at the top.

Unmanaged enterprise tech debt acts as a significant impediment to innovation by diverting resources, increasing complexity, reducing agility, and fostering risk aversion. Organizations that prioritize tech debt reduction and modernization efforts are better positioned to foster a culture of innovation and respond effectively to the dynamic demands of the modern business environment.

Chapter 6

MEASURING AND MANAGING TECH DEBT

Gartner has said that organizations that actively manage and reduce technical debt will achieve at least 50% faster service delivery times.[16] This aligns with the findings of a McKinsey study that some companies that actively manage their tech debt free up engineers to spend up to 50% more of their time on work that supports their strategic business goals.[17] And a 2018 study found that agile practices have a positive effect on the management of tech debt.[18] This chapter provides guidance on how to achieve this goal. **Managing tech debt begins with actively measuring that debt, speaking a common business language to describe that debt, and creating formal processes for influencing and persuading the executive team regarding the prioritization of that tech debt.**

Speaking a Common Language of Tech Debt

Executives understand financial debt leverage. Speaking of tech debt in terms of enterprise tech debt leverage begins to establish a common language through which IT executives can communicate the impact of technical debt with their board and other executives. Unlike financial debt leverage, tech debt has almost always been considered a negative term. Financial debt leverage is a strategic lever that CFOs can utilize to achieve strategic goals. Technical debt is very similar. The difference is that financial debt leverage is actively measured and managed, whereas technical debt is usually lurking behind the scenes, not actively measured, and mostly unmanaged from the enterprise perspective. Speaking of tech debt in terms of enterprise debt leverage helps to create a common language for the CFO and board to understand.

Tech debt could be strategically leveraged in order to build a new solution in the future, but it must be done with full intent of paying off the tech debt in a specific timeframe. Without that intention, tech debt is nothing more than a growing liability. When used as a strategic tool, tech debt can be as much of an asset to a company's strategy as financial debt would be. Speaking of both in terms of leverage helps quantify that debt so everyone can understand when it is acceptable and when it needs additional resources and prioritization to reduce it.

Predicting the future is a thankless effort, but tech leaders regularly find themselves in the role of prognosticators. Given the significant amount of technical debt building up with aging infrastructures, most CIOs and tech leaders are well aware of the growing systemic risk they face, but without addressing the concept of tech debt leverage they are speaking different languages from the rest of their executive team peers. Convincing other executives to address that risk takes great skill in addition to speaking a common language around tech debt leverage. Too many tech leaders are lacking in the art of persuasion and mistakenly think that others see the same risks and simply accept them. The reality is that most other executives don't understand the systemic risk because tech leaders haven't clearly articulated or quantified it.

The first step in managing tech debt is to quantify that debt, as explained in the beginning of this chapter. The next step is to explain that risk in a persuasive manner. For CIOs to do so we must understand our power base.

Finch and Raven defined five bases of power[19] as: (1) coercive power, which is based on fear and the threat of punishment; (2) reward power, which is based on the ability to give rewards or incentives; (3) legitimate power, which is based on formal position or authority; (4) expert power, which is based on knowledge, skills, or expertise; and (5) referent power, which is based on personal characteristics or charisma.

IT executives can use this understanding of different types of power to influence other executives to address tech debt and systemic risk. For example, coercive power would be used when explaining the threat of system failure and potential financial loss. Legitimate power is using their position within the organization to push for addressing tech debt. Hopefully they have both expert and referent power by the nature of their background and the experience upon which they can draw to educate others on the consequences of not addressing the systemic risk posed by tech debt. Misunderstanding their base of power can lead to lack of persuasive arguments for both quantifying and addressing systemic risk.

For a recent example we need look no further than the issues facing Southwest Airlines during the 2022 holiday season.[20] While they were affected by the same winter storms as every other airline, their operations were hit much harder than their competition. Other airlines canceled less than 20% of their flights; Southwest canceled more than 70%. Other airlines recovered in days while Southwest took weeks. Southwest stock dropped by 16%, and they reported over $800 million in loss, including over $400 million in cash. The root cause was pure tech debt; their lack of attention to modernizing their scheduling technology had been a known problem for years. Why was it not addressed? No one was able to make a persuasive case for spending the time and money to fix something that seemed to be working.

Many years ago, I experienced a similar circumstance. I was CIO for a company during an acquisition. As part of our due diligence, I determined that we needed to replace most of the integrating company's hardware. Their systems were not up to our standards, and it was clear that they had extended their upgrade timelines because they knew they were looking to be acquired. It was clear to me that if we didn't replace these systems during our acquisition, we would be forced to replace them in very short order. Replacing them now would make for a much smoother overall transition.

Our CEO did not want to incur the large expense of upgrading the hardware and felt that my assessment was biased. He thought I just wanted everything to be the same hardware because it was "how we do it." I mistakenly thought that I was operating from a base of expert and referent power, but I had not established this level of trust with him yet. He sought out other opinions and found plenty of people who agreed with him that this was not a needed expense at this time.

Eventually we made our cases to the owner of the company. The CEO was clearly operating from his legitimate power base, and the owner made it clear that this was an operational decision and that my role as the tech leader was to implement the technology plan in the way the CEO wanted.

As we began onboarding this company, their systems failed and the transition was quite bumpy. We ended up having to replace all of the hardware just as I had predicted. The operations were significantly affected, and we did not make a good first impression as the acquiring company.

As we were dealing with the operational fallout and unexpected financial costs of this upgrade, the owner came to my office to discuss the situation. I thought he was coming to tell me that he recognized that I had been right, and I was hopeful that this would build trust for future similar situations. I was surprised to find that this was not the case. He made it very clear that I was to blame for this debacle and stated that I should have been more persuasive in articulating the risk associated with ignoring this tech debt. He indicated that I should not have allowed him to decide in the CEO's favor. This was a key learning moment for me. I recognized that being right has no value if I cannot be persuasive.

Acknowledging the level of tech debt leverage across the enterprise is not enough. That knowledge must be followed up with an articulate and convincing explanation of the systemic risk to the business if that debt is not managed.

IT leaders tend to see potential systemic risk long before other executives. The Southwest technology team certainly knew that their system would fail, and that their workarounds would not scale in the event of a large-scale outage. Being right about predicting such systemic failure is not enough. As IT leaders, when we take our seats at the executive table and in the board-room, we need to be right—and persuasive. Understanding the base of power from which we are operating can help us become persuasive strategic influencers.

Quantify Your Tech Debt

As Peter Drucker famously said, "You can't improve what you don't measure."[21] If managing tech debt can provide such significant efficiency gains, it would follow that measuring tech debt is a critical aspect of any successful organization. Unfortunately, most organizations don't know how to measure their tech debt, much less how to actively manage it. As unintuitive as it may appear, measuring and managing tech debt can create a competitive advantage for those who do it right.

Highly tech debt-leveraged organizations find themselves spending considerable time and effort maintaining old systems and working against external headwinds such as looming deadlines for end-of-support, end-of-life, and known security vulnerabilities from out-of-date systems. Thus, one of the critical components of measuring tech debt is the ***supportability of the system***, as measured by the amount of time spent maintaining that system. Another critical component is the ***expected remaining life*** of the specific solution (i.e., has the vendor/manufacturer announced an end-of-life or end-of-support date?). This is an indication of how long the specific technology will be available to you and useful within your enterprise tech stack.

To measure tech debt leverage it would be important to assess each technology within your enterprise tech stack against the following criteria:

- **Business Criticality**: How critical is this particular technology to your operations?

- **Supportability**: How much time and effort does the IT team spend to keep this technology operational?
    - How much babysitting does the system need to meet your regular ongoing operational needs?
    - Are there manual workarounds needed to keep the system functioning?

- Does the system have to be restarted regularly, or are data feeds constantly requiring manual intervention in order to be properly processed?

- **Alignment with the Strategic IT Plan**: Is the technology part of your long-term IT strategy?
  - Are systems or capabilities duplicated within your enterprise tech stack? If so, which one is the long-term strategic solution, and which is being phased out?

- **Expected Remaining Useful Life**: How close to the end-of-life or end-of-support are the various systems within your enterprise tech stack?
  - This is a measure of how much time and effort will need to be put into upgrading those systems or migrating them to another technology. The closer you are to the end of useful life, the more leveraged you would be from a tech debt perspective due to the time sensitivity of focusing the resources on this effort.

- **Stability**: How stable is the technology?
  - What is the uptime of the technology? How often does this system interrupt your business operations?

- **Footprint / Span**: How widely used, and how business critical, is this particular technology within your enterprise?
  - Systems that are limited to a small number of employees, and that are not business critical, would have a

smaller impact on your tech debt leverage. Systems that are widely used and more business critical would have a higher impact on the tech debt leverage.

Rating Definitions

	Tech Debt Rating Category	0	1	2	3	4	5
Operational	**Stability / Fragility**	Stable	N/A	N/A	Unstable	N/A	Fragile/ Brittle
	Supportability	N/A	Easy	Average	Hard	Not Supportable	N/A
	Expected Remaining Useful Life	No defined EOL (yet)	>5 Years	4–5 Years	2–4 Years	1–2 Years	Out of Support >1 Year
	Footprint / Span	N/A	Small	Multi-Department	Enterprise	N/A	N/A
Strategic	**Business Criticality**	Deprecated	Non-critical	Important	Critical	Mission Critical	Foundational
	Alignment with Strategic IT plan	N/A	In Plan	In Plan – Transition State	Not In Plan	N/A	N/A

Figure 1

Using these categories as a basis, it would then be important to quantify each technology in these six areas. A typical scale is shown in Figure 1. The weights and scaling of these attributes should be customized to your unique environment using your organization's risk appetite and transformation goals.

Note that not all categories will have a complete 1-5 rating. Some make more sense as a 3- or 4-level scale. In those cases, use the appropriate rating to achieve the desired weight for each rating in that category. For example, in the "Stability/Fragility" category, a simple 3-level scale makes the most sense. The system is either stable, unstable, or fragile. Given the significant operational impact of a fragile system, it makes the most sense for that rating to be a 5. If a system is stable, it has no effect on tech debt, so it makes the most sense for that rating to be 0. If a system is unstable, the rating could be a 2 or 3, depending on your particular risk sensitivity for unstable systems. In this example, it is rated as a 3 because unstable systems would likely have a larger impact on tech debt.

As the ratings are adjusted, note that for operational items the higher numbers indicate a bad state (i.e., more impact on tech debt). For the strategic items, the higher numbers indicate more business criticality (i.e., larger impact on tech debt). The main idea here is that as these categories are calculated the higher numbers would indicate more tech debt leverage.

The next step would be to normalize the scoring to come up with a single number that objectively quantifies your Enterprise Tech Debt Leverage. To do this, take the sum of the four operational attributes (Stability, Supportability, Expected Remaining Useful Life, and Footprint) and multiply that with the sum of the two strategic criticality attributes (Business Criticality and Strategic Alignment). This is done because the strategic attributes have a greater impact on the potential negative implications of the tech debt and its effect on achieving those strategic goals. Normalize the values by dividing the computed value by the total possible value. This should yield a number between 0-1. Finally, express this number as a percentage. Do this for every technology within your enterprise tech stack. Figure 2 shows an output that would come from using the scale as defined in Figure 1. Now calculate a single Enterprise Tech Debt Leverage number for your entire enterprise using the same normalized calculation (see the Total Tech Debt number at the top of Figure 2). This becomes your Enterprise Tech Debt Leverage data point that you can easily discuss with your executive team and your board.

By way of example, let's evaluate the calculations shown in Figure 2. First, determine the denominator based on your rating scale. The denominator comes from the scales used (see Figure 1). The denominator would be the maximum possible values for each category, which represents 100% tech debt leverage. Since each category has a different maximum value, we need to use the values from the scale to calculate the denominator. In this example the calculation would be as follows: $(5+4+5+3)*(5+3) = 136$. Use this denominator for each technology that you are evaluating for tech debt leverage.

Next, calculate the value of each technology in your tech stack. For Technology 14 in Figure 2, this would be calculated as follows: $(3+3+0+3)*(1+1) = 18$. This is the numerator for determining the debt leverage for this row. Determining the tech debt leverage is then as simple as dividing the technology score against the total possible score, or in this case: $18/136 = 0.13$ (13%). Technology 1 in Figure 2 is $9/136 = .066$ (7%). Repeat this for all of the technologies in your tech stack.

The overall tech debt is then calculated by summing all of the results for each technology and dividing them by the total possible tech debt leverage. For the example in Figure 2, we have 15 items in our tech stack that we are evaluating, so the denominator (100% possible tech debt leverage) is 136*15 = 2040. Adding all of the technologies' scores together gives us 807, so the overall tech debt leverage for the entire tech stack is 807/2040 = 0.395 (40%).

TOTAL TECH DEBT	40%						
Component (Application, Infrastructure, or Vendor)	Tech Debt	Stability / Fragility	Supportability	EOL Timeframe	Footprint (Span)	Business Critical	Strategic Alignment
Technology 14	13%	3	3	0	3	1	1
Technology 1	7%	0	1	1	1	0	3
Technology 12	6%	0	1	0	3	1	1
Technology 13	6%	0	1	0	3	1	1
Technology 5	10%	0	1	5	1	1	1
Technology 15	32%	3	3	2	3	3	1
Technology 7	40%	3	3	0	3	3	3
Technology 9	37%	1	4	4	1	4	1
Technology 3	53%	5	2	1	1	5	3
Technology 4	53%	5	2	1	1	5	3
Technology 11	55%	5	4	5	1	2	3
Technology 10	57%	3	3	4	1	4	3
Technology 8	72%	5	3	5	1	4	3
Technology 2	76%	5	2	5	1	5	3
Technology 6	76%	5	3	4	1	5	3

Figure 2

It is not realistic to target 0% tech debt. You would want to define a scale for your enterprise based on your acceptable tech debt leverage. A common range might be that tech debt leverage less than 40% is acceptable, anything between 50%-70% is concerning, and anything above 70% is critical. Using this framework, you would end up with something similar to Figure 2 as the final output.

In reviewing Figure 2, note that Technology 14 is unstable and relatively hard to support, but it does not yet have an end-of-useful life defined and it does have wide usage across the organization. Additionally, it is not business critical and it is in the strategic IT plan. Because it is low on business criticality and it is in the plan, it carries relatively low tech debt leverage. By comparison, Technology 7 has all of the same operational ratings, but it is business critical and is not in the long-term IT plan. This raises the tech debt leverage for Technology 7 into the yellow category.

Using this framework, you could then combine technologies into various categories, such as consumer-facing, internally-facing, financial systems, etc. You would be able to easily see where you are highly leveraged, and which specific technological components need some attention to reduce that leverage. This creates a framework for measuring and managing tech debt that your board, executive team, and others within the organization can use to understand and visualize the impact of your overall tech debt. This also provides a single ratio of tech debt leverage across the entire organization by which you can measure and manage your tech debt.

The concept of tech debt leverage is a valuable framework that can significantly assist CIOs in effectively communicating and prioritizing their digital transformation activities within an organization. Measuring, managing, and maintaining tech debt, and regularly communicating those activities in the form of tech debt leverage, will help organizations improve their ability to innovate and modernize their infrastructure, data, and systems. It helps them to align technology decisions with business objectives, making it easier to secure support, allocate resources effectively, and prioritize initiatives that maximize the organization's technology investments. This approach not only enhances the understanding of technical debt's impact but also facilitates smoother and more successful digital transformations.

References

1. NPR. (2023, December 18). Southwest Airlines' 2022 meltdown fined by FAA. Retrieved from https://www.npr.org/2023/12/18/1219906471/southwest-airlines-2022-meltdown-fined-faa

2. Holvitie, J., Licorish, S. A., Spínola, R. O., Hyrynsalmi, S., MacDonell, S. G., Mendes, T. S., Buchan, J., & Leppänen, V. (2018). Technical debt and agile software development practices and processes: An industry practitioner survey. *Information and Software Technology*, 96, 141-160. https://doi.org/10.1016/j.infsof.2017.11.015

3. Fillios, Michael C. (2022). Enterprise architecture and tech debt. Architecture & Governance Magazine. Retrieved from https://www.architectureandgovernance.com/strategy-planning/enterprise-architecture-and-tech-debt/

4. Spencer Stuart. (2023, December). Fortune 500 C-suite snapshot: Profiles in functional leadership. Retrieved from https://www.spencerstuart.com/-/media/2023/december/f500-profiles/fortune-500-csuite-snapshot-profiles-in-functional-leadership.pdf

5. Rosenbush, Steven (2023, February 13). Pro Take: CEO leadership is the key to realizing full value from tech. The Wall Street Journal. Retrieved from https://www.wsj.com/articles/pro-take-ceo-leadership-is-the-key-to-realizing-full-value-from-tech-76f97264

6. U.S. Securities and Exchange Commission. (2023, September 28). SEC Adopts Rules on Cybersecurity Risk Management, Strategy, Governance, and Incident Disclosure by Public Companies. Retrieved from https://www.sec.gov/news/press-release/2023-139

7. Clay, Ian and Cory, Nigel (2023, April). Data is not oil, bacon, or gold: An actual measure of data as an asset. Information Technology & Innovation Foundation. Retrieved from https://itif.org/publications/2023/04/03/data-is-not-oil-bacon-or-gold-an-actual-measure-of-data-as-an-asset

8. Knapton, Kenneth. (2020). Exploring mid-market strategies for big data governance (Doctoral dissertation, Walden University). Retrieved from https://scholarworks.waldenu.edu/dissertations/9161

9. ibid

10. Redman, Thomas C. (2016, September). Bad data costs the U.S. $3 trillion per year. Harvard Business Review. Retrieved from https://hbr.org/2016/09/bad-data-costs-the-u-s-3-trillion-per-year

11. BlackLine. (2021, January 20). 70% global business leaders and finance professionals lack confidence in data. Retrieved from https://www.blackline.com/about/press-releases/2021/70-global-business-leaders-and-finance-professionals-lack-confidence-in-data

12. Protiviti. (n.d.). Global technology executive survey. Retrieved from https://www.protiviti.com/us-en/global-technology-executive-survey

13. Omeyer, Alex (2021). The cost of technical debt. DZone. Retrieved from https://dzone.com/articles/the-cost-of-technical-debt

14. CodeScene. (n.d.). Calculate business costs of technical debt. Retrieved from https://codescene.com/hubfs/calculate-business-costs-of-technical-debt.pdf

15. Blumberg, Sven, Das, Rahul, Patenge, Rob, Lansing, Jens, Motsch, Nils, & Münstermann, Björn (2022). Demystifying digital dark matter: A new standard to tame technical debt. McKinsey & Company. Retrieved from https://www.mckinsey.com/business-functions/mckinsey-digital/our-insights/demystifying-digital-dark-matter-a-new-standard-to-tame-technical-debt

16. Gartner. (n.d.). How to assess infrastructure technical debt to prioritize legacy modernization investments. Retrieved from https://www.gartner.com/en/publications/how-to-assess-infrastructure-technical-debt-to-prioritize-legacy-modernization-investments

17. Dalal, Vishal, Krishnakanthan, Krish, Münstermann, Björn, and Patenge, Rob (2020). Tech debt: Reclaiming tech equity. McKinsey & Company. Retrieved from https://www.mckinsey.com/business-functions/mckinsey-digital/our-insights/tech-debt-reclaiming-tech-equity

18. Holvitie, Johannes, Licorish, Sherlock A., Spínola, Rodrigo O., Hyrynsalmi, Sami, MacDonell, Stephen G., Mendes, Thiago S. Buchan, Jim, Leppänen, Ville (2018). Technical debt and agile software development practices and processes: An industry practitioner survey. Information and Software Technology, 96, 141-160. https://doi.org/10.1016/j.infsof.2017.11.015

19. Mind Tools Content Team. (2020). French and Raven's five forms of power. Mind Tools. Retrieved from https://www.mindtools.com/abwzix3/french-and-ravens-five-forms-of-power

20. Hicken, S. (2022, December 31). How Southwest Airlines landed itself in a computer mess. The New York Times. Retrieved from https://www.nytimes.com/2022/12/31/opinion/southwest-airlines-computers.html

21. Drucker, Jacob (2018, December 4). You are what you measure. Forbes. Retrieved from https://www.forbes.com/sites/theyec/2018/12/04/you-are-what-you-measure

About the Author

Dr. Knapton is a veteran technology leader with broad experience in IT operations, software development, enterprise architecture, software design, program management, project management, analytics, infrastructure, quality assurance and user interaction. He applies his vast experience in his role as CIO to improve under-performing IT organizations and specializes in teaching IT organizations how to be agile, and how to establish a service-oriented IT culture. Dr. Knapton holds 3 patents for his early work on enterprise security and anti-virus technology and has published a book on family safety and technology. Dr. Knapton earned his doctorate in IT with his dissertation on big data governance. He also holds a Master of Business Administration from Brigham Young University, a Master of Science with a focus on Strategic IT Leadership from Walden University, and a Bachelor of Science in Computer Science and Information Systems from Utah Valley University.

www.ingramcontent.com/pod-product-compliance
Lightning Source LLC
Chambersburg PA
CBHW050513210326
41521CB00011B/2443